**Errata:**

Page 29, 1st paragraph. Ballyshannon Extension was the second last section to be built.
Page 30, end of paragaraph 2. (Lataigh – the muddy, mirey place)
Page 31, 2nd paragraph. "...a sign for the Sand House Hotel."
Page 32, 6th paragraph, insert after second sentence.

"Approximately half a mile further on, the line crossed the road for the final time to begin its long loop into the station."

## LONGINGS

*I long to stand where the sea birds call,*
*And watch the great waves break and fall;*
*For there's life on the hills and life by the sea,*
*And voices forever are calling to me*
*From the wilds of Donegal*

quoted from an excursion arrangements publicity leaflet issued by the
County Donegal Railways Joint Committee for the summer season of 1957

## *A brief note about maps.*

New 1:50,000 Ordnance Survey maps are now being issued by both the OS of the Republic of Ireland and the OS of Northern Ireland and are far superior to the old half-inch series as they both now include the routes of old railways. We certainly recommend buying them. Map nos. 10, 11 and 16 cover Donegal.

With luck our little thumbnail sketches will make some sort of sense when you compare them to the real thing!

# DONEGAL'S RAILWAY HERITAGE

**By way of an introduction**

As you travel through the beautiful glens of County Donegal the last thing that you expect to discover is evidence of an extensive railway network. But that's exactly what this guide aims to show you — a railway system which reached out to many of the little towns and villages for more than a hundred years.

Well within the memory of local people, steam trains and diesel railcars pounded up and down the valleys bringing essentials such as coal, foodstuffs and Guinness, and carrying away the fish from Killybegs, cattle and sheep from the farms and, always with sorrow, emigrants to the waiting ships in Derry. And, of course, the railway carried children to school, their mothers to the shops and their fathers to work. Many people with relations in Co. Donegal still recall regular annual journeys on the railway bringing them westwards to spend their summer holiday with an aunt or uncle.

All in all, for decade after decade, the County Donegal Railway provided an essential local transport service that linked this remote and magnificent part of Ireland with the rest of the rail network. Further north, the Londonderry and Lough Swilly Railway performed the same vital job and, as the roads and available vehicles improved, both companies gradually moved away from railway operations and transferred their transport functions to buses and lorries.

The Lough Swilly traded in its trains for buses in the 1940s and the CDR eventually followed suit in 1960. In 1971 the CDR company's buses and routes were absorbed into Bus Éireann but the Lough Swilly Co. survives to this day and you can still travel on their distinctive vehicles around the north of the county.

This guide, the first of three, covers the majority of the railway lines operated by the County Donegal Railway; those from Stranorlar-Ballybofey to Donegal, Killybegs, Ballyshannon and Glenties. The second in the series will cover the lines from Strabane to Stranorlar-Ballybofey, to Letterkenny, and to Buncrana and Carndonagh. The third guide will deal exclusively with the Lough Swilly's Letterkenny to Burtonport Extension Railway which ran right across north Donegal.

**The coming of the railways**

Railways first came to County Donegal in 1863 when a group of leading local landowners and businessmen in the lower Finn valley met and decided that the new invention of steam rail transport would greatly assist in improving the prosperity of the area and bring the advantages of cheap transport for local produce.

The Great Northern Railway of Ireland had already arrived at Strabane. Its line came northwards from Enniskillen, through Omagh and Strabane and continued along the western side of the Foyle valley to its terminus at Foyle Road Station in the Maiden City. The GNR(I) line continued southwards on from Enniskillen and, eventually, gave rail access to Belfast and Dublin, and the

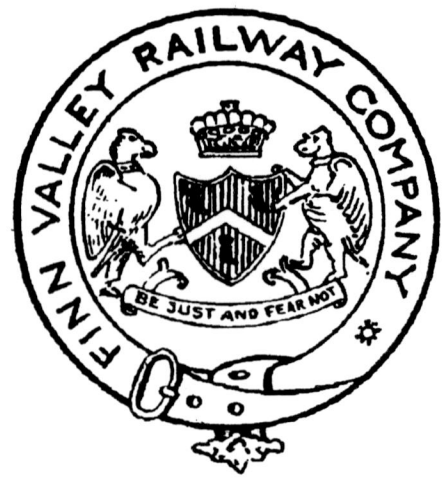

many towns between. This useful route, connecting Strabane with three important Irish cities — all markets and seaports, was an ideal stepping-off point for further railway expansion and the obvious route led westwards into the productive farmland of the eastern part of County Donegal. And so a company, the Finn Valley Railway Co., was established and built. Starting from Strabane it followed the River Finn upstream via Clady, Castlefinn, Liscooly and Killygordon to Stranorlar-Ballybofey.

Within a few short years expansion westwards was underway with the formation, construction and opening of the West Donegal Railway in 1882. Westwards past Lough Mourne, over the high turf boglands and through *an Bhearnais Mhóir,* the Barnesmore Gap, to Donegal Town. However not everything was easy. The money ran out while they were still just past Lough Eske, several miles short of Donegal itself, and passengers had to resort to horse and carriage to complete their journey. It wasn't until several years later, in 1889, that the railway pushed on into Donegal.

Ireland's main railways were built to the country's standard gauge of five-foot three-inches, this being the gauge (the width between the rails) of the GNR's line at Strabane and of the little Finn Valley Railway to Stranorlar. The West Donegal Railway, however, decided on a narrower gauge as more suitable for scaling the heights of the Donegal highlands and built theirs to the narrow gauge of three feet. This resulted, in the early days, in a change of gauge — and train — at Stranorlar.

Amalgamation came in 1892 and the gauge of the Finn valley line was converted to three feet, moving the change of train to Strabane, at the company's junction with the GNR. Also, by this time, the government was promoting the development of the infrastructure of the so-called "congested districts", that is those areas of Ireland where it was felt there was insufficient farmland and other employment to support the local population. As a consequence, two important branches were built using government subsidies. The first ran on from Donegal Town along the northern shore of Donegal Bay to the busy fishing port at Killybegs, while the second stretched from Ballybofey along the upper River Finn valley to Fintown and on to its terminus at Glenties. Killybegs was reached in 1893 and Glenties in 1895.

Further consolidation took place and, by the time the GNR and the Belfast and Northern Counties Railway moved to jointly take over the railway in 1906, branches had been added which ran south from Donegal to Ballyshannon, north-west from Strabane to Letterkenny and, finally, northwards from Strabane on the east side of the River Foyle to give the CDR its own terminus at Victoria Road, Derry. At its furthest extent the lines operated by the County Donegal Railways Joint Committee (as it became in 1906) totalled an amazing 124 miles. Of this 46.25 miles were the main line from Derry to Donegal and the rest comprised four lengthy branches.

It was a complex system with Ballybofey-Stranorlar at its centre. The first two decades of this century were the heyday for the "Wee Donegal". Well patronised and always efficient the railway provided the vital transport infrastructure for this rural corner of Ireland. After the First World War came Ireland's war for independence from Britain and the country's subsequent partition. Twenty-six counties of the country, including Donegal, formed the Irish

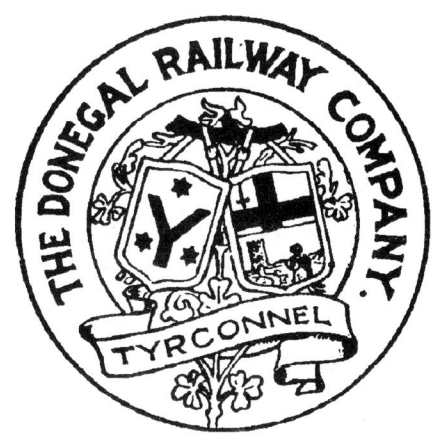

Republic, while the other six counties remained in the British empire as part of the United Kingdom. A lengthy and winding border cut south from Derry to the eastern borders of the Blue Stack Mountains and then, after several convolutions, turned eastwards and meandered round Tyrone and Fermanagh, Armagh and Down to reach the Irish Sea near Newry.

All the railways that ran entirely within the new Éire became nationalised into the Great Southern Railway. All those entirely within the new Northern Ireland became the property of the Ulster Transport Authority. The County Donegal, along with the Lough Swilly and several others, crossed the new border — some repeatedly — and so remained independent.

CDRJC general manager Henry Forbes pushed forward with improvements and during the 'twenties and 'thirties a new fleet of petrol and diesel railcars was built up to gradually replace all passenger steam workings apart from excursion and holiday specials.

The railway was the first in the British Isles and only the second in Europe to introduce diesel vehicles and was highly innovative in their use. The first railcar, (No. 1, of course!) was, however, petrol engined and was purchased in 1907. It was a compact four-wheeled vehicle built by Messrs Allday & Onions of Birmingham and originally intended to be used purely as an inspection car. However, it soon proved its worth as a mail carrier and in emergencies when a steam loco failed. There was further pressure to move towards internal-combustion engined vehicles arising from the British coal strike in 1926 and, soon after, Henry Forbes was looking around to buy a few bargains from other railways.

The early railcars were a very mixed bunch but were able to handle an increasing number of the timetabled trains. The fleet was expanded by converting buses at the GNR works at Dundalk and others were bought from the Clogher Valley, Dublin and Blessington, Derwent Valley and Castlederg and Victoria Bridge railways.

This move into petrol and diesel railcars certainly extended the life and flexibility of the railway and during the 'thirties, 'forties and 'fifties it continued to operate in fine form. Various road vehicles were acquired at different times and, by the time of closure in 1959, the CDR was one of the major hauliers in the county.

## The going of the railway

However, the realities of economic life could not be kept at bay forever and complete closure of the railway services took place in the last day of December, 1959. It was the end of an era. The next day buses in the familiar red and cream livery of the railway took over passenger services and lorries now carried the goods over the whole journey.

The rails were ripped up, the station buildings were sold and the engines, railcars, carriages and goods wagons put up for auction. Many vehicles found new uses as farm stores, garden sheds and one, a railcar trailer, was bought by Donegal Football Club for use as the ticket office! Some of the steam engines went for scrap but others went to Belfast Transport Museum along with the CDR's unique diesel tractor *Phoenix*. Other locos, railcars and carriages were sold to an American dentist but he went bust and they never left their native land. Now in widely-different states of repair these locos, *Drumboe, Columbkille, Meenglas* and *Blanche,* form the centrepieces of the preserved CDR rolling stock in various museums in the north of Ireland.

**But not dead, just resting!**

Now, apart from the various sites covered in this guide you can see the remaining County Donegal Railway engines and vehicles at the Foyle Valley Railway Centre in Derry, the Belfast Folk and Transport Museum's magnificent new railway hall at Cultra, the SDRRS's depot in Donegal Town and, on long-term "holiday", railcars 19 and 20 at Douglas, Isle of Man.

About one mile of three-foot gauge track has been relaid on the old GNR trackbed in Derry and is well worth a visit.

The South Donegal Railway Restoration Society is committed to re-opening a steam-operated line and we have Class 5 loco *Drumboe* to restore as well as a variety of rolling stock on which we are already working. We have even saved railcar no.15, officially scrapped in 1961 and in use as a holiday home in the north of the county since then, and we intend to restore her back to full working condition. And we've "saved" Trailer no. 5—she'll also be restored to running order.

The CDR is a railway that just won't go away! Cutting through magnificent scenery and linking pleasant and picturesque towns and villages it has bequeathed to us a heritage of industrial and social history which brings the landscape to life and gives the visitor a deeper and more profound appreciation of this beautiful part of a beautiful country.

# *Deora Dé*
# The Tears of God

One of the most delightful sights to the visitor to County Donegal is the wild Fuchsia growing just about everywhere.

These beautiful plants were introduced to Ireland from their native South America sometime in the eighteenth century and, like so many other visitors to this magical island, fell under its spell and set up home here. Now you can see their descendants throughout the country, whether you are in Kerry or Cork, Galway or Mayo, Antrim, Down, or here in Donegal.

The wild fuchsias are of the single variety and, soon after their introduction (perhaps as ornamental plants in the gardens of some of the great houses) they began to spread across the countryside and colonise any suitable, reasonably protected spot — although having said that you'll find these attractive shrubs clinging on in some of the most windswept and weather-beaten spots of the Atlantic seaboard.

Where they do get protection from the wind they can grow very high — for a fuchsia! Hedges 10 or 12 feet tall are not uncommon and there are some memorable stretches of road where the fuchsia hedges on either side form a dark green and crimson corridor down which you can drive.

And it wasn't just the fuchsias that fell under the spell, the people here immediately admired their resilient nature, deep green leaves and striking, pendulous red flowers and christened them *"Deora Dé"* - the Tears of God.

# Donegal Town, the Glengesh Pass, Glenties, Fintown, Ballybofey, Stranorlar, the Barnesmore Gap, Donegal Town

**Tour One**
*Circular, day tour*

Our first tour begins in Donegal Town, *Baile Dún na nGall* (the town of the fort of the foreigners), and on foot! You should leave your car and walk from the Diamond up Tirconnail Street past the Post Office on the left until you come to a small cross-roads. Directly over the road from you is the old entrance to Donegal Station. Although it looks complete when viewed from this side this fine two-storey building with the single-storey extension is almost all that remains of a once extensive station layout. Walk up the approach road as far as the hall on your right for a better view of the building. **Please note:** this is now a *private* access road used by Bus Éireann, *you must not proceed any further.* The two-story building was

Donegal Town Station—the Agent's House

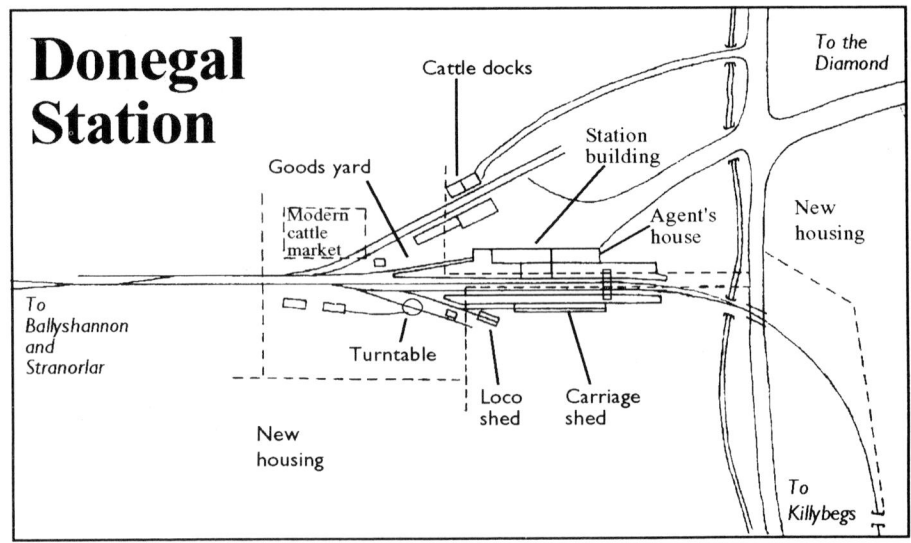

the agent's house—he was the local representative of the railway and responsible for all its affairs in the area. The single-story section to the right comprised the original booking office, waiting room and other facilities, it is now used as an office and rest room for Bus Éireann crews. Facing these buildings across the yard are several light industrial structures occupying the site of the original railway goods yard. Retrace your steps back to the cross roads and turn right and then right again so that you can view the original platform side of the station. Be careful though, the platform has been cut back and the narrow roadway is used by lorries and cars heading for the cattle market beyond the station site *and there is only very limited clearance.*

Walk up this roadway until you are at the far end of the station and look back. This is the view that trains from the Barnesmore Gap and Ballyshannon would have had in approaching the station. The remains of the old engine shed can be seen in the community centre yard to the right. All other structures have now disappeared.

The original through route continued past the platform, over the road and then curved below the housing estate through what is now a sports field and running track around to the right and under a road overbridge. Walk back to the road and look across. You can make out the sharp right curve and the remains of the road bridge in the near distance. It's worth noting that the now demolished station at Killybegs was of a very similar design to that at Donegal, although comprising only two gables (as indeed did Donegal itself until enlarged to accomodate the station master's family).

Now walk back to the Diamond and get in your car. Take the road signposted for Killybegs, *Na Cealla Beaga* (the little churches), the N56, heading westwards. You are in fact retracing the route of yet another branch of the old railway but we'll leave its exploration to another day. About a mile short of Killybegs look for and take the rightward turning towards Ardara, *Ard a' Ratha* (the height of the fort). About seven miles along this mountain road watch out for the left-hand turning signposted for Glencolumbkille, *Gleann Columbcille* ([St.] Columbkille's glen).

This is the Glengesh Pass, *Gleann na Geise* (glen of the sprite [taboo]), in the valley of the river of the same name. Take the road right up to the top until you are well past the summit, watch out for a turning to the right and use this to carefully turn around. Now take the road back down the Pass and pause at the vantage point after the hairpin bends to enjoy the view. In the distance is Aghla Mountain, *Eachlach* (possibly, a place of steeds, horses) above Glenties, *Na Gleanntai* (the glens), and beyond is Slieve Snaght, *Sliabh Snacht* (the snowy mountain) and the Glendowan Mountains, *Gleann Doimhin* (the deep glen [the mountains of . . .]).

To the left is Gweebarra Bay, *Gaoth Barra* (Barra's inlet), Dungloe, *An Clochan Liath* (the grey stone), and the Rosses, *Ros* (a promontory, i.e. place of many points). Off the distant coast is Aranmore, *An Árainn Mhór* (the big Áran [arched back]). Travel back down the road and turn left onto the N56 heading through Ardara and to Glenties.

Glenties Station can be reached from the village by walking down Main Street in the Dungloe direction. At the head of the town there is a fork in the road. You should take the right-hand road (signposted Fintown, Letterkenny), and travel past the new comprehensive school, on your left for about a quarter of a mile.

The station house and goods shed are now visible on your left, down the original station approach road and behind the hedge

The water tower (without the tank), and engine shed are still standing. Interestingly the turntable well is also still in existence, the only CDR example to survive. However the cattle pens, the carriage shed and, of course, the tracks themselves are long gone.

Please note that Glenties Station building is now a private residence and permission *must* be obtained from the owner before visiting. *Please do*

9

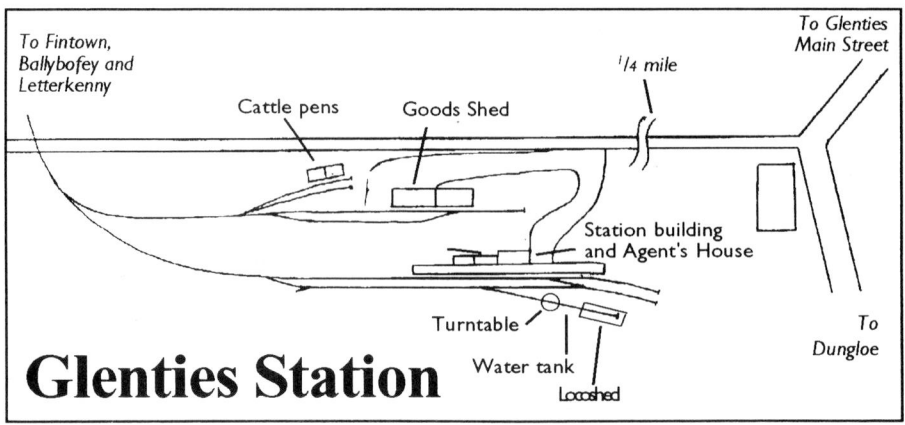

not trespass. There is a good collection of CDR items on display in the Glenties Community Museum nearby.

The Glenties branch was often the location in the 1920s and '30s for the early petrol-engined railcar operations although they operated over the whole system in the heyday of the railway's working. Now is the time to pause for morning coffee. Why not call into the Highlands Hotel for this? On the left, down the Main Street.

After coffee travel along the main street and turn right at the end onto the R250, signposted for Fintown, *Baile na Finne* (Finne's town) and Ballybofey, *Baile Bó Féich* (the town of Féich's cows) or *Bealach Bó Féich* (the way/road/pass of Féich's cows). We are now about to trace the route of the old County Donegal Railway's branch from Glenties. Stretching some 24 miles up through the mountains the Glenties branch, although closed for passengers in 1947 and for everything else in 1952

has survived as well as the trackbed high up in the Barnesmore Gap, *an Bhearnais Mhór* (the big gap or pass). The trackbed appears and disappears alongside the road at a number of points to the right of the road as it winds its way down the Finn valley, but can be clearly seen, and then we are in Fintown, *Baile na Finne* (Finne's town).

The station, still standing, lies beyond the village and down to the right towards the shore of Lough Finn. It is in good order and of the "large cottage" type typical of the more remote points of the old CDR empire. The goods shed here is the base for the re-opening of another railway in Donegal, this time by the *Cumann Traenach Gaeltacht Lár*. Onwards and eastwards the little places pass, Bellanamore, *Béal an Átha Móir* (the

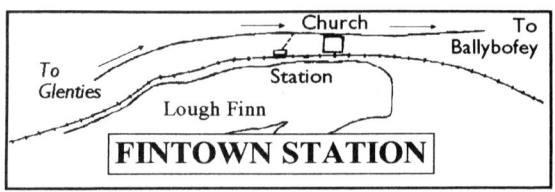

10

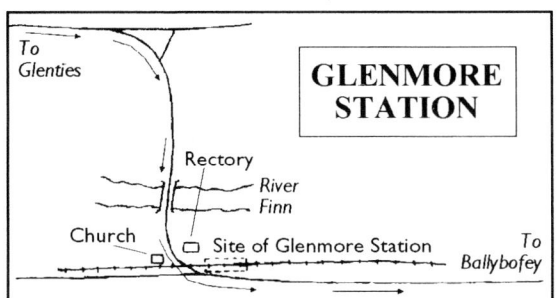

mouth of the big ford), Glassagh, *Glaise* (the place of many streams), Elaghtagh, *Aileachta* (the place of many stone forts/houses), Cloghan, *Clochan* (stepping stones, i.e. a ford), Glenmore, *An Ghleann Mhór* (the big glen), all railway halts in their day. The mountains close in as our route (the R252) twists and turns down the little valley — an epic setting for a railway even though there were always only a very few passengers to carry, the most profitable traffic was cattle carried in market-day specials.

At Glenmore, as you cross over the River Finn, the station site was on your left-hand side just after the bend in the road. It is now a county council yard. Behind you, you can clearly see where the line ran just beside the small Church of Ireland Church. Further on towards Ballybofey a local farmer has made ingenious use of an overbridge, by turning it into a shed!

And so, after many miles of Donegal mountain scenery we finally arrive at the Twin Towns: Ballybofey and Stranorlar, *Strath an Urláir* (river holm of the level place), divided by the River Finn. Stranorlar was the original headquarters of the old County Donegal Railway and the Twin Towns Chamber of Commerce have played a vital part in the work of bringing the trains back to Co. Donegal. Ballybofey is now the busier of the two and it is to be connected with the new South Donegal Railway at Meenglas, *Mín Glaise* (the mountain meadow of many streams), by a special vintage bus service for passengers.

As we enter this typical Donegal town the N15 joins us on the right, having come up through the Barnesmore Gap. The railway had a halt in Ballybofey, on the Glenties branch, but the main junction station was over the river in Stranorlar. For the moment drive on through Ballybofey and cross the River Finn bridge and pause near the church on your left. The entrance to Stranorlar Station was on the other side of the road. Unfortunately there is now nothing left to see of the fine and distinctive buildings which once stood here. It is now the site of the Bus

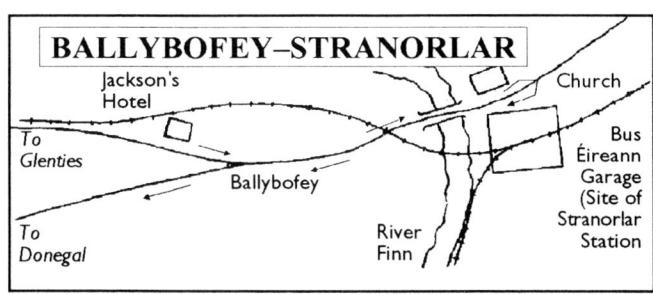

11

Éireann depot and only the old stone perimeter walls give any indication of its original use. The modern utilitarian steel-clad block is on the site of the old decorative building which, perhaps unique in public buildings of the time, sported a remarkable clock tower built over the gents lavatory!

The building survived until the mid-1970s as the central depot of the railway company's freight and passenger road services but was demolished entirely when the company was taken over by CIE. Only the clock itself now survives and is the subject of much discussion—where should it be placed?

Now you need to turn around and make your way back to Ballybofey, continue along the Main Street until you see the signpost for the L75, which we have just travelled down. And it's surely lunch time! So, having turned off the main road go a short way and then look for the entrance on the right to Jacksons Hotel where lunch is to be recommend.

Jacksons is a real institution and you will receive good hospitality here — the hotel is a sponsor of the railway restoration project and has had more than a passing acquaintance with the old railway.

If you happen to get a window table in the dining room looking out over the rear lawns then you have a grandstand view of what was once the old railway line of the branch from Stranorlar to the Glenties!

There was even a short siding off the line leading into the hotel premises where wagons of coal could be delivered ready to be emptied down the shute and into the boiler-room for the hotel heating. The main hotel bar, the counter in fact, was built on the site of the old station house which stood on this site.

Suitably refreshed we are now ready to enjoy travelling along one part of the old railway's main line and, perhaps, the most spectacular part of it — the Barnesmore Gap. Turn back to the road junction near Jackson's Hotel and take the right-hand turning onto the N15 signposted for Donegal and Sligo.

Having left the station at Stranorlar, the main line to Donegal Town swung intially south before crossing the River Finn and swinging southwestwards to being the long climb up to the summit of this section at Derg Bridge, nearly 600 feet above sea level.

As you travel along the N15 the line is hidden away up to your left running through farmland. Soon the conifer plantations of *Coillte Teo* (the Irish Forestry Board) appear along the road and gradually the road and railway routes begin to converge.

At the top of McGroary's Brae the long stiff climb past the stone schoolhouse at Meencarrgagh (*Min Carraige*—the rocky mountain meadow) the line re-emerges through a deep cutting to run parallel once more with the road and the head of Lough Mourne.

It has been said that the railway was responsible for reintroducing the beech tree to Donegal and indeed those plants set as lineside hedging survive to this day. By picking out the beeches you can easily identify the course of the line on this southerly end of the system.

Stranorlar Station — sadly, now demolished

It's worth stopping here at the head of the Lough to take in the view. Before you lies the stretch of water which St Patrick cursed and to this day holds no salmon! Beyond this you can trace the line as it heads to the Derg Bridge, past which lies the famed Barnesmore Gap (*An Bearnais Mór*—the big gap or pass). An awe-inspiring sight—on a clear day, of course!

And if it *is* a fine day, why not leave your car and take a short walk up to the Lough Hill to enjoy the view. (See sketch map overleaf) Simply follow the rough road past the county council's pump house and, ignoring the first right-hand track, continue on up to the hill and turn along to your right. This track actually continues around to meet another road which crosses the Derg Bridge but, as you still need your car, you'd better retrace your steps.

Back on the main road and heading south a single span stone bridge soon appears. This is the Derg Bridge, complete with platform. This halt was opened in 1912; a 400-foot siding was put in here in 1946 to transport locally-quarried sand and gravel to Ballyshannon for the Erne dam scheme at Assaroe. Just back from the Derg Bridge a single span miniature bridge carries the line over the *Sruthán Dearg* — the little red stream. The road bridge is known as the Red Burn Bridge.

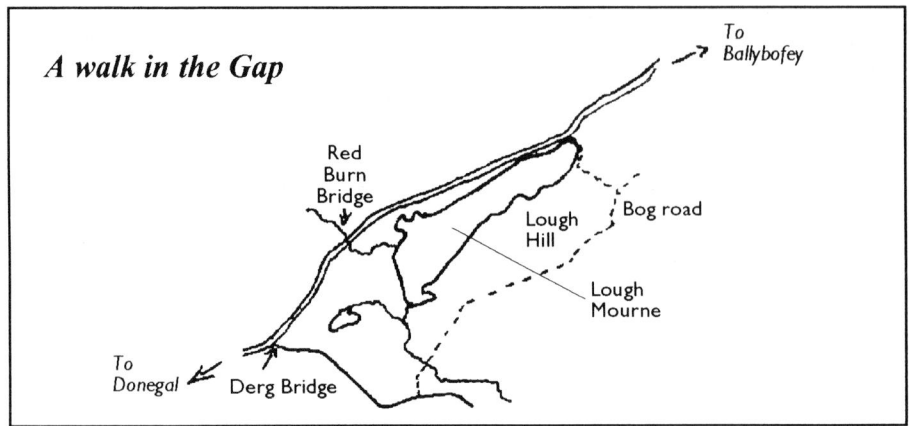

## A walk in the Gap

The Barnesmore Gap is before us and the road and railway keep close companion as they both cut a path through this dramatic scenery. Then the railway trackbed travels over to the left-hand side of the Gap while the road keeps to the right. Another plantation obscures the railway's route but you can make out an indentation in the tree tops near the lower border, this is the indication of the trackbed, still used as an access way by the foresters. We journey onwards, south-westwards through the Gap with only the occasional sheep and fellow motorist as our companions. The trackbed is clearly seen — you can make out the sharply-defined ledge cut into the granite mountainside to our left. Note the beautiful retaining wall at the south-west end of the Gap, a tribute to the skill of the engineers and builders.

We now reach that famous local landmark, Biddy O'Barnes bar, on our right. We shall pause here to get our bearings — and maybe a pint or two! The car park is on the left-hand side of the road.

St Columbkille prophesied that the end of the world would be heralded by *An Muc Dú* (the Black Pig) racing through the countryside. So it was little wonder that the first train to run through here in 1882, hauled by a black locomotive (the then livery of the CDR) was regarded with deep fear and suspicion by some of the older inhabitants. Indeed, many watched its first passage through the Gap from the heights of Croaghconnellagh (*Cruach Connailach*), the mountain to your right—about as near to the new-fangled railway as many felt it safe to be. The mountain on your left is Croaghonagh (*Cruach Eoghanach*).

A good look at the surrounding countryside gives you an idea of the construction problems facing the railway and explains why, when they got just beyond this point on their way to building the track on to Donegal the money ran out and they had to settle for a temporary terminus at Druminin, *Drumínann* (ridged land — very apt!). In the eighteenth and nineteenth centuries, before the coming of the railway, the Barnesmore Gap was the lair of highwaymen and robbers who used to prey on the stage coach as it made its way along the old road on the other side of the valley from the railway trackbed. You can still see the odd section of roadway cut into the opposite hillside and this remained the only route through until the coming of the trains and, much later, the new road on which we are travelling. Now back to Biddys for a reviving drop (though not for the driver, of course!) and then drive on down the road towards Donegal Town to complete the circle.

Approximately two miles down towards Donegal town, where the road widens, is Lough Eske halt, conveniently situated opposite a telephone box! This was the site of that original terminus for passengers destined for Donegal town, built when money ran out in 1881. Passengers then continued their journey by horse and car until 1886, when the West Donegal Light Railway Order empowered the company to raise £19,000 to complete the line into the town.

The line crossed the road here and for the next two miles ran on your left again, and can still be traced. Where the road widens again note the crossing house immediately to your left. About half-a-mile further on, just before St Agatha's Church at Clar, the line crossed for the final time and continued its journey on into Donegal Town, meeting the Ballyshannon branch just behind the hospital.

As you travel through the gentle countryside of this seaward fringe of the mountains you might like to recall the many railway journeys of the past along the same route and the many that are to come when the steam trains come back to County Donegal.

"Biddy's o' the Gap"

# Turf:
## the fragrant fuel

Visitors often remark that there seems to be something magical in the air of Ireland, and of Donegal in particular. Part of that magic must be the arometic scent of turf fires wafting through the breeze.

There's nothing quite like a turf fire to really add to the coziness of a room, whether it's a cottage parlour, hotel lounge, welcoming bar or the most sought-after corner of the tea-rooms. Winter or summer it brings its atmosphere of warmth and well-being to every location.

But, like any other fuel, that enjoyment has to be won at a price.

Throughout Donegal you'll notice the long lines of the turf cuttings running across the high moorlands. Little tracks snake away from the road to end abruptly in a stack of plastic sacks and mounds of the brown drying turf.

Donegal's turf comes from "blanket" bogs of sphagnum moss and each cutting (turbery) is the prized possession of its owner.

Hand-cut turf is dug using a special spade, a *sleán*, which allows long slivers to be cut and placed on the top of the bank. The pieces of turf are then stacked up three or four at a time for the first part of the drying-out process. As the moisture begins to leave them they are stacked in successively larger mounds until they are ready to be sacked up and transported.

At home, the turf is then carefully restacked in great heaps and covered with a waterproof sheet or thatched over to keep the rain out. Turf—the fragrant fuel!

# Donegal Town, Killybegs, Carrick, Teelin, the cliffs at Slieve League, Donegal Town

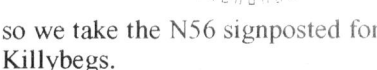

**Tour Two**
*Out and back full-day tour*

Our second tour is along the scenic south Donegal coastline following the course of the old railway's Killybegs branch, *Na Cealla Beaga* (the little churches). Once again our starting point is the Diamond in Donegal Town and we are going to trace the route of the track as it disappeared under the road overbridge that we noticed when we visited Donegal Station in Tour One.

The track swung right around the town and then headed out to the west and so we take the N56 signposted for Killybegs.

Travelling on the Killybegs road, about one-and-a-half miles out, turn right at the Opal Garage (O and I Motors) and continue on up to the next junction, at the end of the houses. As you turn left, in the bushes you'll see the remains of no. 9 crossing cottage,

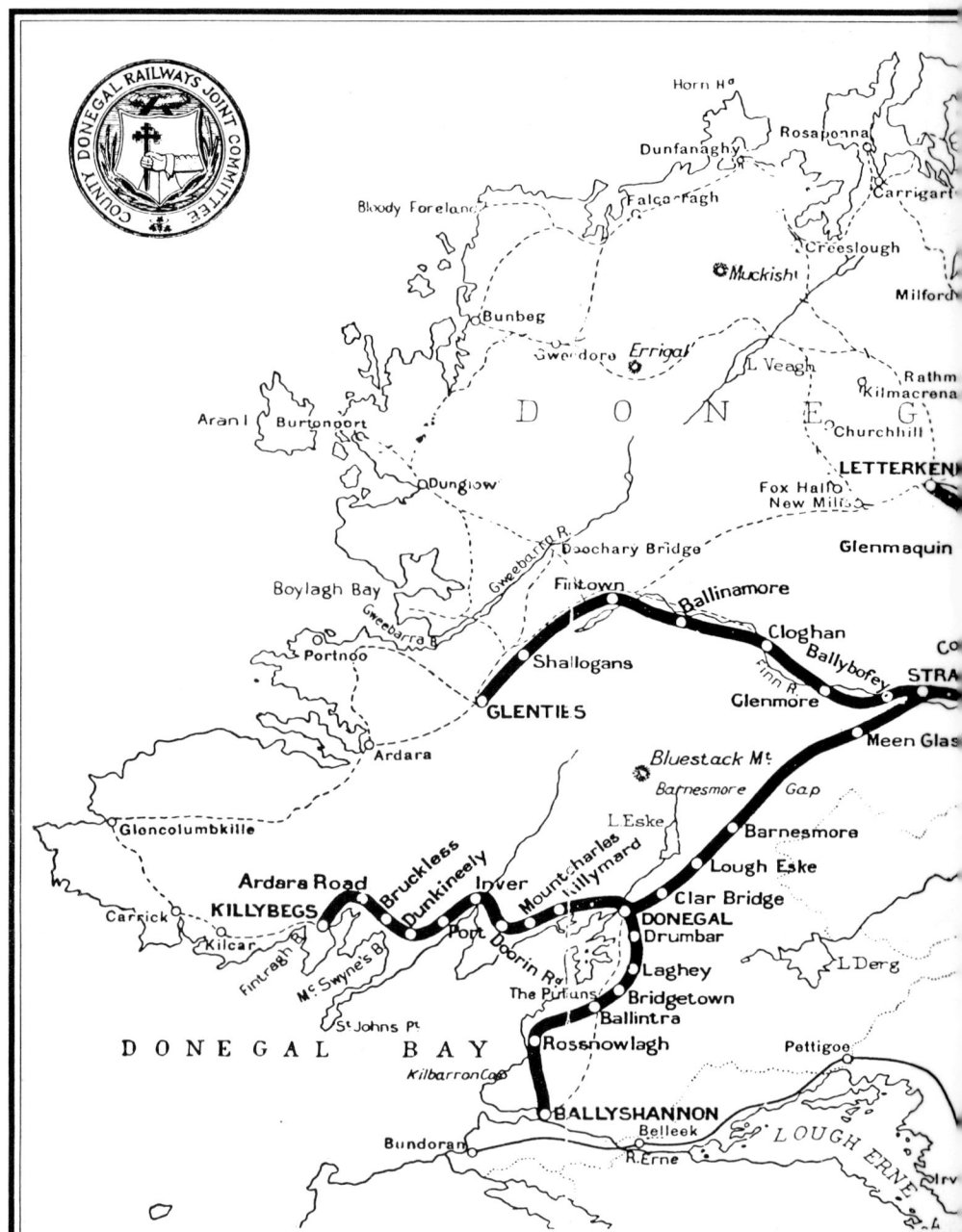

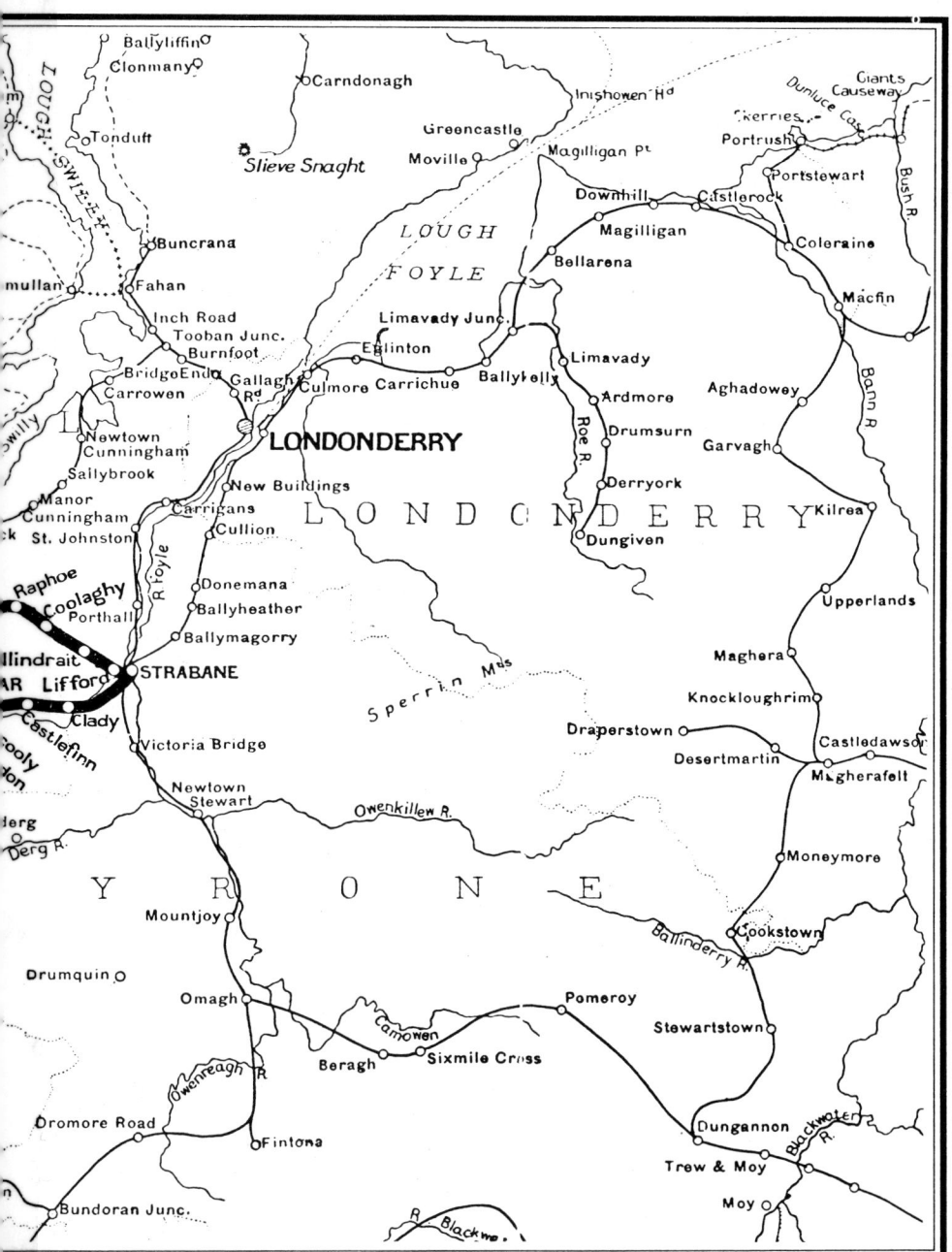

McGroarty's. The line runs parallel to the road on your right and soon you reach Bogle's Crossing (no. 10). Until recently here stood one of the last intact wooden crossing gates, this is now in the Society's ownership and undergoing restoration.

Continue along the road, to pass under the double-arched bridge at Dromore. Turn right to rejoin the main road at Keeney's Crossing (no. 11). Killymard Halt was just back from here to your right. Now turn right.

As we proceed westward we are in drumlin country. The whole of this part of Ireland was covered in a massive glacier during the last Ice Age and the ground was crushed under an enormous weight. As this weight moved southwards it carried forward great masses of rocks and stones which, when they came across particularly large and immovable masses of rock projecting up were piled up against them and left behind

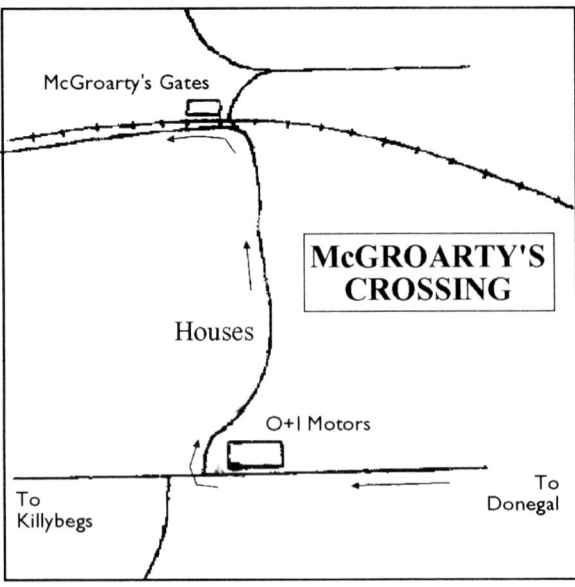

by the glacier.

When the ice melted these characteristic hump-backed small hills were left dotting the landscape. They are much longer than wide and all "point" in the same direction—along the movement axis of the glacier. This means that, as we are moving westward, and the glacier moved southward, we are constantly crossing these little hills and climbing up and down the steep-sided valleys scoured out of the landscape by the advancing ice.

The railway, of course, needed to keep gradients to an absolute minimum and so the line out to Killybegs twisted

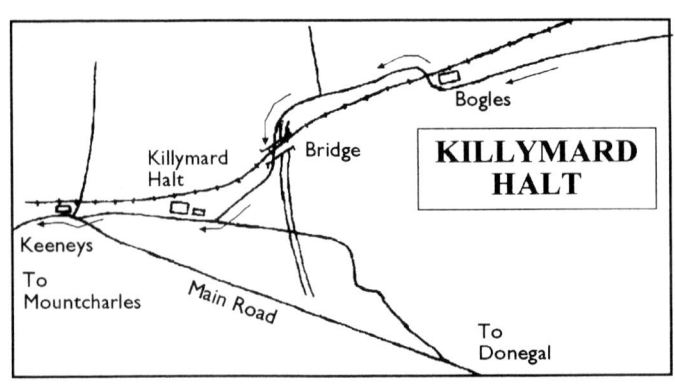

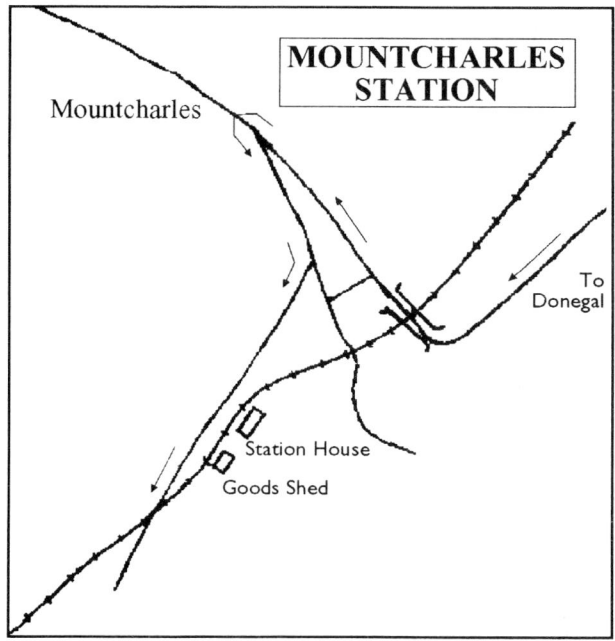

Mountcharles, *Tamhnach a tSalainn* (the salty arable fields).

Coming into Mountcharles you cross over a road bridge and the station buildings can be seen away to your left. Take the second left (at the school patrol sign) and then the first right and this will bring you along to the station, now a *private* house. Note the Goods Shed, still in use. The line crossed just west of the shed and can be followed along by road to the next junction.

Turn right at the junction and go up to the next crossroads; note the crossing keeper's cottage on your right — Freeburn's (no. 13). Turn left and follow the road along for almost a mile to the next crossroads. On your left here is Doorin Road Station, *Dú Rían* (the black path?), now a *private* house. You are now at the summit of the Donegal-Killybegs branch at 201 feet. From here to Inver, *Inbhear Náile* (St Naul's river mouth), the line wheels backwards and forwards across the road.

Turn to your right here and continue along, through the second Keeney's Crossing (no. 15) and Mullanboy (no. 16 — Rose's Gates) to rejoin the main Donegal-Killybegs road at Inver Bridge. If you stop just past the bridge and look north Inver Station appears behind the school, with the goods shed and platforms

and turned like a writhing snake to try and keep something like level. Even so there were main spots where the trains had to drop down a hillside and then climb a steep bit of track to get up the next one.

When it was still running, back in the 'forties and 'fifties, the railcars often couldn't climb the gradient and so had to run backwards, then reverse again, pick up speed and charge the hill!

With their rather inadequate springs this often meant a lively ride and on at least one occasion caused a passenger to break his false teeth as the railcar hit the bottom and everyone was thrown upwards as it churned up the rise. The trackedbed is visible occasionally on the right-hand side of the road as we proceed towards almost unchaged since CDR days. It is, again, a *private* dwelling now. Visible also are the bridge abuttments where the line crossed the river. If you detour a short way up the road past the station and stop at the bridge, look to your left and you'll see one of the only four water towers left on the whole system — this one is completely intact and still holds water as if waiting for the next thirsty train!

Returning to the main road follow it to the next village, Dunkineely, *Dún Cionnaola* (Cionnala's fort). From Inver the line crossed from the right to the left of the road by an underbridge which was just at the top of the hill a quarter mile further on. As you climb the hill away from the station turning you can see Lappin's crossing house (no. 24) in the hollow to your right. The railway crossed under the road just here.

The line then continues alongside and parallel with the road and to your left. At the next crossing house, McMenamin's (no. 25), it veers away

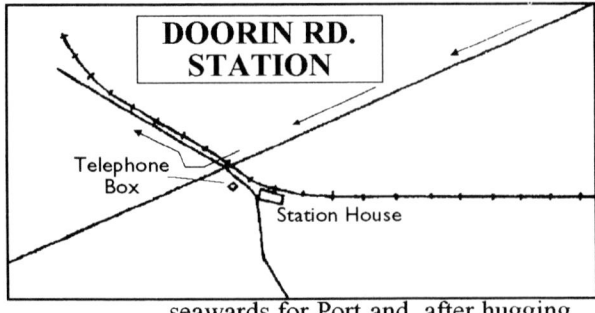

seawards for Port and, after hugging the coast for over a mile, comes back up to rejoin the main road again. In fact it *is* the main road at this point, rounding Seahill before dropping to cross the Bunlacky river over a typical double-arch bridge before striking away across country to Dunkineely Station. To see the station, turn left as you reach the start of the town and it's about half-a-mile down on your left.

From here the line snakes across the rolling fields to the north of St John's point and comes back to the main road just before the small village of Bruckless. As you turn the sharp bend before climbing up the village, note the bridge in on your left.

Bruckless Station is set back off the road to your left just past the garage and shop. As you climb the hill out of the village, the line crossed again under the road an as you gain the twisting flat road further on you can see the embankment parallel on your right running through a beautiful wild valley. Further on watch out for the second McMenamin Crossing house (no. 27) just up a

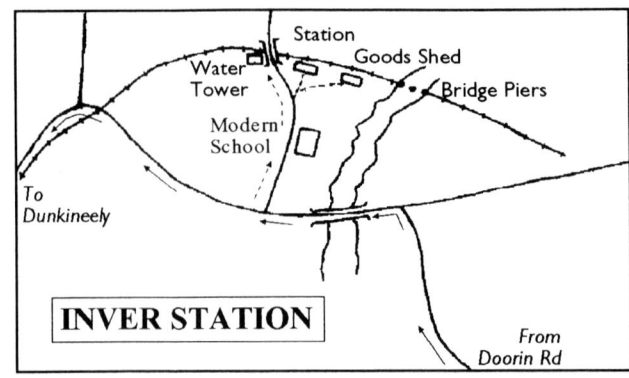

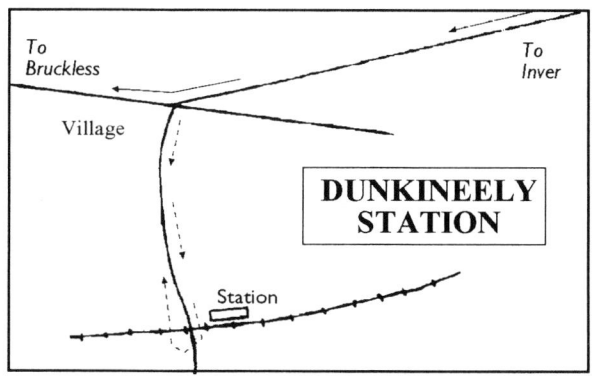

by-road to the right, opposite the Glen Stone Quarry.

At the end of a long straight, the main road veers sharply left; Ardara Road Station is up on the right. Yes, this *is* the road to Ardara, *Ard an Ratha* (height of the fort), but you'd better have a pony and trap waiting because Ardara itself is about seven miles away to the north!

The line now curves away from sight as it makes a southward turn to run towards Killybegs, one of the finest natural harbours in Ireland and a great centre for the fishing industry. It rejoins the main road as you approach the outskirts of the town. Having crossed the lough head watch for the parapet of a bridge just past the fish factory — the large industrial building to your left — here the line crossed under the road for the last time and ran down along the shore to its final destination. This modern plant replaced the original factory and you always knew when you were near Killybegs when travelling by railcar because you could smell the fishmeal being processed. Great stuff for the farmers of course but not exactly Chanel no. 5!

Past the factory the railway kept to the sea wall and terminated in a fine

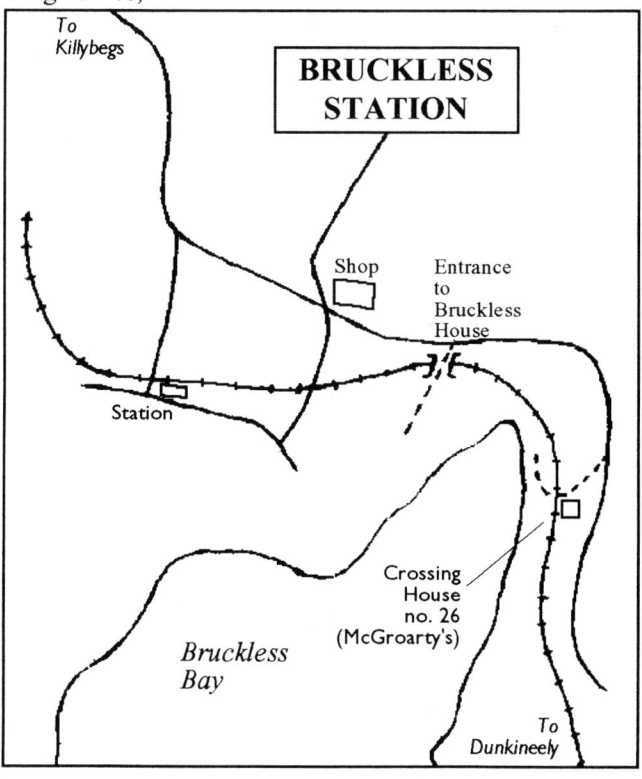

station situated just before the Pier Bar on the left-hand side of the road as you enter Killybegs town. Drive past the Pier Bar and turn to the left to park.

Walk back along the sea wall and you should be able to spot a curved wall and semi-circular flowerbed. This is all that is left of the station, it is the site of the old turntable which iteself was made from the underframes of a withdrawn steam engine — Henry Forbes didn't believe in throwing anything away!

The station building was a two-gabled version of that still standing in Donegal and also had a large overall roof that covered most of the platform and the railway lines which the passenger trains used. And it was needed. The wind and rain blow in hard here and the passengers were very welcome of the protection when they arrived at this, the most westerly point on the system. As in most of the other station sites in the larger towns nothing now remains of the terminus buildings.

Killybegs is a delightful town as well as being an important one. You can see the new buildings belonging to the fisheries, and the boats tied up from their work way out in the North Atlantic. There are some very big fishing boats based here and the industry was always important in the days of the railway.

Now turn back and walk towards the car park but keep to the quayside. The old fish pier stretches out to your left and protects a poignant reminder of the days when the steam trains ruled. Walk onto the pier and you will see two lines of metal buried into the tarmac with just their tops showing.

You are now looking at, walking

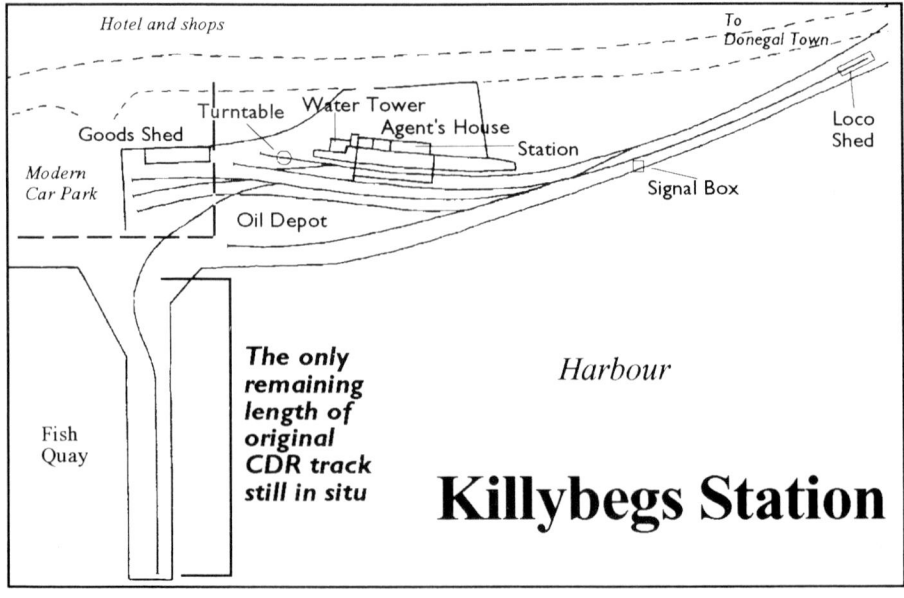

## Killybegs Station

on, the only surviving pieces of County Donegal Railway track still in situ! Several goods lines went past Killybegs Station and continued on along the quayside to an oil terminal, and one cotinued in a tight curve onto the fish pier itself.

In years gone by the boats tied up here and the fish boxes were loaded into vans ready for a quick start behind a steam engine in top condition. Maybe it was *Drumboe*, or *Meenglass, Owenea* or *Blanche* that pounded away out of the town early in the morning to speed the fish to the markets of Belfast and Dublin. Speed was essential, not just to ensure freshness but to win the best prices possible against the competition from the other fishing ports around Ireland.

Many fish suppers eaten in Irish cities started their journey behind a steam engine at Killybegs. And talking of fish suppers, lunch calls! So why not enjoy the real thing and cross over the road to Mellys and enjoy a real fish and chips lunch — we recommend it.

Over lunch you might like to consider the optional addition to this tour or simply decide to spend a few hours in one of the pleasant bars enjoying the view and a drop or two of the black stuff.

**Optional extra half-day tour**

The optional extra half day we suggest is something of a "what if". When the railway was built out to Killybegs in 1893 there was some talk of taking it on still further westwards to the "government" fishing pier at the remote village of *Teelin*.

Now, the members of the SDRRS are great enthusiasts for the railway and its part in the history of County Donegal but even we must admit that this would have been quite a remarkable scheme.

If built the extension would have rivalled many of the Swiss mountain railways for landscape—and their gradients! If the route to Killybegs had been rather bumpy, that beyond would have been positively dynamic.

Our afternoon trip begins from the car park in Killybegs. Take the road signposted for Kilcar, *Cill Charthaigh,* (St Cartha's church) and Carrick, *An Charraig* (the rock) westwards out of the town and follow its course uphill. Keep to the main road as it swings right and drops down to Kilcar.

Watch out here, the steep drop down through the village suggests the main road goes straight on but we need to turn right to keep on the road to Carrick.

This high road has a pleasant surprise along the way: a beautiful view of the Teelin estuary down below to the left with the broken skyline of the summit of Slieve League behind it.

There's another inconspicuous turn to make at Carrick. Drive through the main street until you see a sign for a left turn to Teelin (just before the bar and hostel on the left, and opposite the shop on the right), and take that turning. Follow this road right along through the village.

Slieve League, *Sliabh a Liag* (the mountain of the flagstones), rises to almost 2,000 feet to your right while, to your left the Glen River (excellent fishing) gradually widens out into an estuary and Teelin Harbour. Drive right on to the end of the road at the pier.

If you look across the estuary you can see the proposed route of the railway extension around the bottom of the hills which you have just driven over. It would have swept right round from seaward, up the estuary, crossed the river then followed the road right up to the pier.

Now retrace your path and drive back through the village until you see the signpost pointing leftwards up to Slieve League. Turn left here and follow the road right through to the little hamlet of Bunglass, *Bun Glaise* (the bottom of streams, i.e. where they fall into the sea),where there is a gate across the road. You can either park here (please don't obstruct the roadway) and continue for about another mile on foot along a magnificently set road or you can stay in the car and drive right on up!

You'll soon see some of the tremendous views southwards right across Donegal Bay to Benbulben and the mountains of Sligo. Keep on going until you reach the car park at the end. You are now looking at the highest sea cliffs in Europe! The pathway leads onwards from the car park right on the very edge of the cliffs to the aptly-named One-Man's Pass. The latter part of the route is a steady climb and don't forget to mind your step. The view is worth the walk and the photos you take will be a reminder of this beautiful part of County Donegal's wild scenery.

Make your way back down. We recommend a reviving draught in *The Rusty Mackerel* in Teelin village — its collection of jugs and Guinness signs (*ás Gaeilige* of course) and warm hospitality make it a welcome sanctuary after the walk up Slieve League.

Now, back to the car and travel back towards Carrick. Turn right down the main street then bear right again just after the bridge. This takes you on to the minor coast road along the other, eastern, shore of the Teelin estuary and back to Kilcar. Again, at Kilcar, take the right turn as you climb up the main street to take that minor road which follows the coastline round to rejoin the main road just west of Killybegs. This more or less follows the projected railway route. Then continue back into Killybegs and the main road home to Donegal.

The cliffs of Slieve League

## Doing it by Bus!

It's quite possible to see and enjoy most of Tour One by bus and on foot. It just needs a little re-adjustment.

We recommend using Donegal Town as your base and devoting a separate day to each section. This will give you a wider and even more leisurely view of things and, of course, everyone can enjoy the local hospitality without worrying about the driving.

The first section of Tour One is just a short walk from the Diamond to the old Donegal Town Station.

Section two begins by returning to the town centre and taking the 10.45am Bus Éireann local service to Ballybofey. This heads eastwards out of Donegal up through the Barnesmore Gap on the main road to Letterkenny and Derry.

Depending on how long a walk you'd like to take along the old railway line either ask the driver to drop you off at the old quarry road at the top of the Gap or at a suitable point somewhere along the loughside towards Meenglas. You'll see the old railway trackbed to your right. Just join it wherever you like and walk back towards Donegal Town. The trackbed is still private property so please make sure that you close the sheep gates as you go. Just beyond the Gap itself you'll go through a short cutting and then you'll come to a path heading back to the main road. The bus stop is back at Biddy's and the local service comes along at about 3.30pm.

Section three will take us to Killybegs. Again, we start from the bus stop outside the Hyland and Abbey hotels at the Diamond. The service leaves at about 10.30am and Brian's bus will get you to Killybegs at about 11.15am. Along the way watch out for the old railway's route as it crosses and recrosses the road. The return bus picks you up again at about 1.45pm and gets you back to Donegal Town at 2.30pm.

If you want to go out to the cliffs at Slieve League then you should stay on the outward bus and stay overnight in Carrick at the hostel or a B&B. This will give you plenty of time to walk out to Teelin and then out to the cliffs. The buses to Donegal pass through Carrick at about 8.45am and 1.15pm.

Unfortunately, you can't travel along the upper Finn valley by bus but it is possible to visit Glenties and spend a pleasant hour or two in this lovely town. There is a bus from The Diamond at about 9.30am that goes through to Glenties, the return is at about lunchtime. Please check locally for the times.

Tour Three is also a bit awkward. There are plenty of good buses from Donegal to Ballyshannon but they take the main road. Check local times and, combined with a bit of walking, you should be able to see quite a few of the sites (and the sights!).

It *is* possible to backpack all the routes. Many of the villages have hostels and there are plenty of B&B places, though you will need to book in advance for dates during the high season.

And there are a number of places that rent out bicycles so, all in all, you needn't be restricted to travelling by car or bus.

Details can be obtained from the local Bord Fáilte offices—see page 40 for addresses and phone numbers.

# Donegal Town, Laghey, Ballintra, Rossnowlagh, Ballyshannon, and return

**Tour Three**
*Out and back full day tour*

The Ballyshannon extension was the last section of the CDR to be completed and was opened on the 2nd September, 1905, having taken two years to construct. The line ran southwards from Donegal Town through rolling hills and grasslands, passing Laghey, Ballintra and Rossnowlagh to its terminus in the northern outskirts of Ballyshannon. This section contains a large number of over and under bridges, all of them a spectacular testament to the skills of their builders and worthy reminders of a mighty railway!

Our journey begins again at The Diamond. Take the N15 for Ballybofey and turn right opposite the hospital onto the old Laghy road. It was at this spot, on the 29th August 1949, that a serious head-on collision occurred. Railcar no. 17, on its way down to Ballyshannon met an up goods drawn by Class 5 loco *Owenea* at the Hospital Halt. The railcar driver and two passengers were killed and many other injured.

The line runs to the left of the road

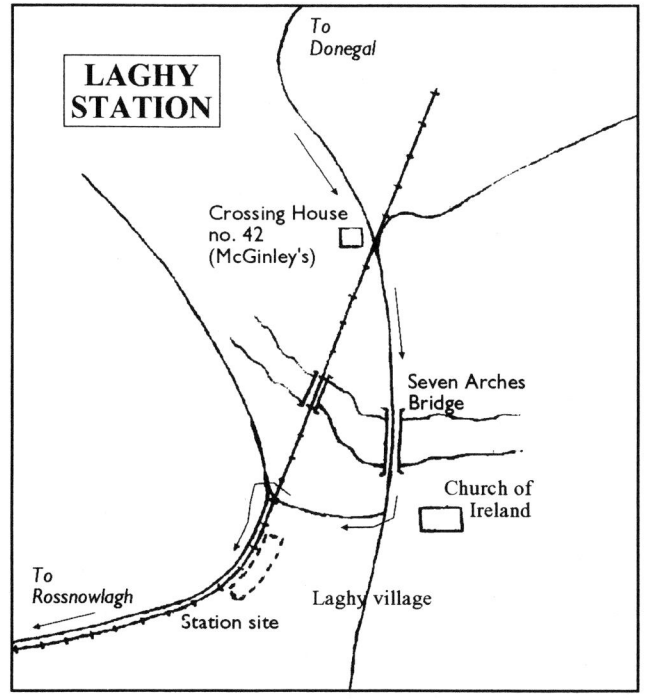

29

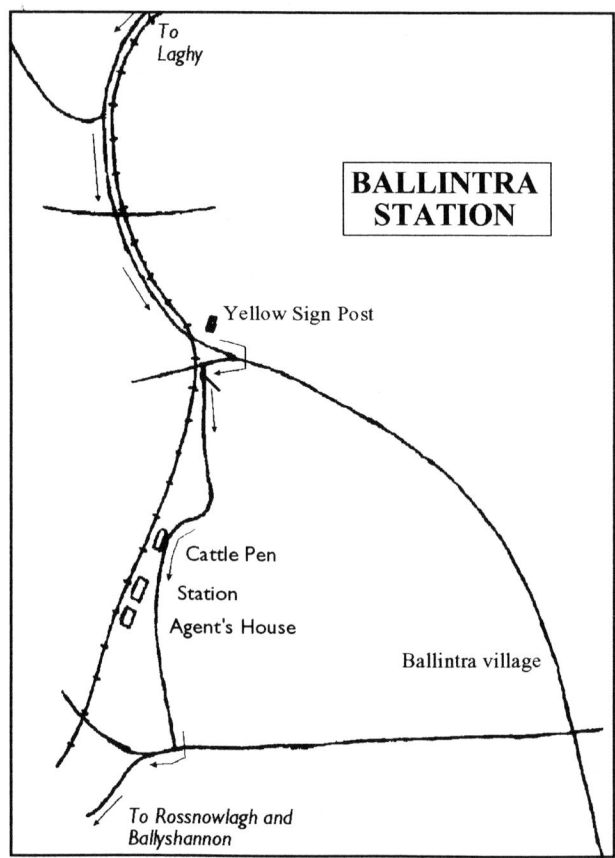

Resuming your journey, about 200 metres further on, the road swing sharp right and in front of you is McHugh's Crossing house (no. 41). Continue on to Laghy (*Lathaigh*—the ruddy, mirey place).

The line now on your left, the embankment being visible at many places. As you round the last corner before the village you cross the line at Monaghan's Crossing (no. 42).

Note the fine stone pillars on your left, one complete with gate hasp, and on your right the high embankment heading out for the main road.

Cross the bridge, turn right and then left onto the main Donegal-Ballyshannon road. Where you are now was where Laghy Station once stood. Behind you the line was carried high over a river by a single-span bridge, the end of the embankment being marked by an advertising hoarding.

For the next three miles or so you are actually driving along the route of the line. Three points of note as you proceed are Conaghan's Crossing house (no. 43), the Carrick Cut — a cutting made through a small limestone knoll, marked by the rock bank on your left, and, just up the

and is visible at various points, though it is rapidly disappearing with land clearance and house building. The first two overbridges are just off your route, up the first and second left turns. The third one you actually drive over, just before the Presbyterian Church at Raneany (*Rath nAonaigh*—the fort of the fair/fete). It's worth stopping here at the church and walking a few yards back along the road. In on the opposite side, the line, having crossed from left to right, is carried high over a river by a fine single-span bridge and is worth a look.

road, Bridgetown Station house. This house, now a *private* residence, is the only house along the road side on your left.

Continue along the main road and follow the sweep to your left. As you climb the hill, keep a sharp eye out for a sign for the Strand House Hotel (yellow board on your left). Turn right at the next crossroads just immediately above the sign and stop; in front of you now you see the remains of the abutment walls of the bridge once here. Turn left. At the next junction carry straight on through i.e., the right-hand road.

The line, now on your right, is visible at various points as it runs down to Ballintra Station. As you go round a left-hand bend, stop where the hedge (on right) is low. Below you, you can pick out the remains of the cattle pens and siding. The station house is now well-secluded in the trees and is a private residence. As you drive down this road you can see the embankment, heavily wooded now, and you can still pick out the telegraph poles, some still bearing the insulators.

At the next T-junction turn right. You are now on the road to Rossnow-lagh. The line remains on your right but crosses under the road about a quarter-of-a-mile from the last junction, just before the two-storied stone-fronted house.

Running now on your left it keeps fairly close to the road. Note the crossing gates and pillars as you proceed. Another quarter mile further on the line begins a long climb to cross a by-road by a very fine under bridge at Glasbolie (*Glas Buaile*—the green booley or grazing place).

The line and road now part company for about half-a-mile but as you round a bend and pass St John's Parish Hall and church you can pick it up again high on your left. Another fine over-bridge can be seen just past the Hall. Gradually the line sneaks back parallel with the road to run along into Rossnowlagh Station. (*Ros Neamhlach*—the worthless headland[!]) The station house is the

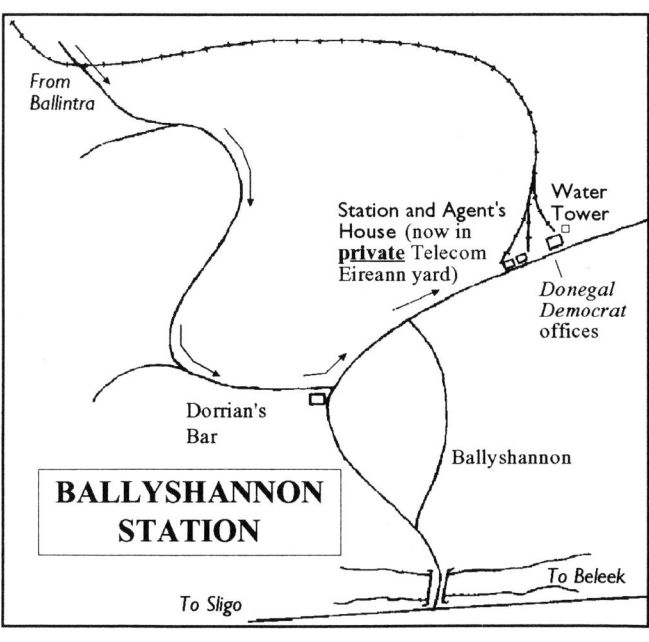

yellow-painted single storey building on the left.

Here was the stopping point for many thousands of holiday makers on their way to the broad strand about a mile off; here the engines could "rest" after the arduous haul of twelve or more coach trains up and down from Strabane.

Resuming your journey road and rail merge at various points for the next quarter mile or so and there's another fine bridge to be seen on your left just below Rossnowlagh Station. Watch out for the telephone box on the right-hand side.

The owners of the house opposite have made an ingenious use for the end of the cut embankment — even Henry Forbes would have approved of this flower bed! From just past this point spectacular views of the coast of south Donegal open up across the bay.

Three-quarters of a mile (or thereabouts) further on the line, hidden away to your left, crossed to the right-hand side of the road via a deep cutting and you pass over the remains of the overbridge, only one of its parapet walls remaining.

For the next two-and-a-half miles or so the line can be seen here and there, weaving through the small hills, passing under the by-roads and eventually coming back to run beside the main road, just past the turn for Creevy, (*Craoibaigh*—the place of many-branched trees. Surely this name best sums up the full might of the Atlantic gales that batter this coast. As so often in Irish this is a very precise meaning and describes the low, stunted trees of this area.)

Further on from the Creevy turn a very picturesque overbridge can be seen next to the road, on your right. On your left you can still make out the trackbed as the line heads first eastwards before turning south towards Ballshannon (*Béal Átha Seanaigh*—the mouth of Seanaigh's ford) and entering the station itself.

Here we must part company with the line for a short while. Continue on into Ballyshannon, turning left at Dorrian's Bar back onto the main Donegal road. Go along to the end of the terrace of houses on your left until you reach a single-storey building clad in grey sheeting.

This was Bally-shannon Station and the two-storied building just beyond it was the agent's house. The yard and the station building are now *private property* and used by Telecom Éireann as a depot.

If you wish to visit the terminus station you must first visit the Telecom office and obtain permission from the depot supervisor. Further up the road the offices of the *Donegal Democrat* are built on the site of the station yard; the sidings and cattle pens were on open ground behind the next row of houses.

The only other reminder of the site's former use is the water tower, standing, minus its tank, in a field beside the *Democrat's* offices.

Ballyshannon can offer plenty of places for rest and recreation to refresh yourself before the drive back to Donegal. Further on, of course, is Bundoran, the terminus of a long winding branch of the old Great Northern, abandoned many years ago — but that's another story!

# Destination: Donegal!

Travelling to County Donegal is all part of your holiday and we want you to enjoy every moment of it.

There are a number of ways of getting to this wild and remote outpost of Europe and below we give some tips that you may find useful.

## By air

County Donegal has its own airport at Carrickfinn, near Dungloe, on the western coast. Flights from Glasgow serve this airport.

Further south there is Sligo airport which has regular connecting flights with Dublin and, therefore, all European cities, and services to the United States.

Even further south is Shannon airport with its regular transatlantic services. To the east there is the City of Derry Airport with services to Glasgow; Belfast International (Aldergrove) with hourly flights from London and regular services from several other British cities and with flights from the rest of Europe; and Belfast City Airport with services from Britain and a growing list of direct connections with Europe.

Car hire can be arranged either with your airline operator (*Aer Lingus*, for example, provide several fly-drive packages) or when you arrive at Dublin, Shannon or Belfast. Shannon airport is 282km from Donegal.

## By sea

Car ferry services operate between Stranraer and Cairnryan to Larne (north-east of Belfast), and by high-speed Seacat hydrofoil right into Belfast's Donegall Quay; to Dun Laoghaire (south-east of Dublin) from Holyhead; to Rosslare (in Co. Wexford, on the south-eastern corner of Ireland) from Fishguard, Pembroke, Le Havre and Cherbourg; and to Cork (Ringaskiddy) from Swansea, Roscoff and Le Havre.

There are a variety of operators and it is well worth getting your travel agent's advice and shopping around to get the best deal. If you're prepared to take a late evening or early morning sailing there are some real bargains. It is essential to book well in advance as all the services are well used.

## Getting there

Once you're on Irish soil then it's fairly straightforward travelling to Donegal.

*From Larne* (190km) take the A8 signposted for Belfast and, just after Ballynure, look for the signs for the M2 motorway. Take the motorway and stay on it until it's end just west of Randalstown and then follow the A6 all the way to Derry. Cross the River Foyle in Derry via the new road bridge and follow the signs for Letterkenny.

After crossing the border checkpoint at Bridgend (*Welcome to Donegal!*) take the N13 and, before Letterkenny, take the N56 down to Stranorlar/Ballybofey. After that it's the N15 through the Barnesmore Gap and on to Donegal Town.

***From Belfast International (Aldergrove)***, (170km) by hire car, follow the exit route past the checkpoint to the main road junction and look for the A26 towards Antrim. Travel through Antrim and follow the signs to the M2. Then follow the route as above.

***From Belfast City Airport*** by hire car, simply follow the signs directing you towards the City Centre and the M2. After negotiating a fairly tortuous series of road junctions you'll arrive at the York Road entrance to the M2, then as above. By the way, as you cross the River Lagan you'll see the new railway bridge uniting the old GNR/BCDR Belfast Central Railway with the isolated section of NIR running from York Road to Larne and due to be opened shortly.

***From Dun Laoghaire*** (225km) follow the signs for the M50 and Lucan and look out for the turning onto the N4. If you miss it, turn back and try again because this is the road that is going to take you right across Ireland. Once on the N4 take it through Maynooth, Mullingar, Longford and Boyle on into Sligo. Here you want the N15 signposted for Donegal and Derry. Sweep northwards with Benbulbin Mountain to your right and, just south of Bundoran, you enter Co. Donegal. Just stay on this road for Donegal Town.

***From Dublin Airport*** (200km) by hire car, from the exit follow the signs for Blanchardstown and the M50 to the west of the city. Once on the M50 look for and take the junction for the N4 and follow the route as above.

***From Rosslare*** (389km) it's quite a run! Follow the signs to Wexford. This will, eventually, get you on to the N25. Just west of Wexford look for the N80 signposted for Enniscorthy. Follow this road through Enniscorthy, Bunclody, Carlow, Stradbally, Portlaoise, Tullamore and Clara to its junction with the N6 at Moate. Take the N6 westwards to Athlone then look for the N61. Take this and follow it through Roscommon, Tulsk and Boyle where it joins the N4. Follow this through to Sligo and then it's as above. Donegal is just over the mountains and the Atlantic is to your left.

***From Cork (Ringaskiddy)*** (408km) follow the signs to the city centre which you'll just have to navigate through. You're looking for the N20 signposted for Mallow and all points north. In Cork city there is an extensive one-way system so if you need to stop and ask then you're looking for John Street Upper and Watercourse Road (the first leads into the second, and both are the N20). Once successfully on the N20 take it through Mallow, Ráth Luirc, Croom and into Limerick. Another city centre to negotiate! Look out for the signs to Ennis and Shannon Airport. These will take you onto the N18 which you follow right through Ennis and Gort practically into Galway. Before the city though, at Oranmore, take the N64 which leads to Claregalway and the N17. Now stay on this road through Tuam, Claremorris, Charlestown, Tubbercurry and on into Sligo. Then head for the northern mountains as above. *Donegal, at last!*

***From Shannon Airport*** (282km), by hire car, its easy! Take the exit road to Hurlers Cross where you can join the N18 and then follow the route as above.

## By train and coach

*Via Larne* you can travel to Derry by Northern Ireland Railways and then take the scheduled Bus Éireann services for Sligo and Galway as far as Donegal Town.

*Via Belfast International Airport* take the Airbus to the Europa Bus Station for Ulsterbus coaches to Donegal via either Derry and Letterkenny or via Enniskillen; or stay on the Airbus to Central Station and take the NIR service to Derry and then by coach to Donegal.

*Via Dun Laoghaire* the excellent DART (Dublin Area Rapid Transit) electric train will take you to Dublin city centre and you can then pick up the bus link from the Central Bus Station (Busaras) in Store Street to Heuston Station. The train can take you to Sligo and there you can join the Bus Éireann Derry service in the station forecourt. This travels up the main road northwards to Donegal Town. Alternatively, you can travel by an express Bus Éireann service direct to Donegal which you can pick up at the quayside at Dun Laoghaire.

*Via Dublin Airport,* again take the Airbus to the Central Bus Station and proceed as above.

*Via Rosslare* your best bet is to travel to Dublin by train or coach and follow the details above. If you want to really experience Ianród Éireann, though, check the times beforehand and catch the daily train towards Limerick via Limerick Junction (a classic railway junction for enthusiasts with its rail-rail level crossing) and then transfer to the Cork-Galway coach, then on to Donegal via the Derry coach.

*Via Cork* you can either travel north-east to Dublin by train or coach and then as above or take the Cork to Galway Bus Éireann express service and change at Galway bus and train station for the Derry express service, as above.

*Via Shannon Airport*, there are airport bus connections with the Cork-Galway express coach service at Limerick as well as at least one Galway service (and on to Donegal via the Derry service) which calls in at Shannon.

There are many special travel deals available and you should check with your travel agent for the best value and convenience. It's well worth investing in a Bus Éireann 7 or 14 day travel ticket.

These are reasonably priced and can cover all your travelling in Ireland, including your initial travelling to Donegal. They vary in extent: bus and coach; bus, coach and rail; Irish Republic only; Irish Republic and Northern Ireland.

It's our experience that if you first find out the cost of your travelling from your point of arrival in Ireland to Donegal, and then use the first day of your travelcard to cover this, and your final return journey, then it really helps to keep costs down.

These tickets must be obtained from Bus Éireann via your travel agent *before* entering Ireland.

Finally, with regard to buses, coaches and trains, it is *essential* that you get timetable information before you book. Make sure you buy the Bus

Éireann timetable booklet, usually published during May of each year. Special summer-only services operate from about the end of May to early September so it's important to check up. The drivers, guards and other staff of Bus Éireann, Iarnód Éireann, Ulsterbus, Belfast Citybus and NIR are very helpful and patient so don't be afraid to ask. Also Bord Fáilte and the Northern Ireland Tourist Board offices are always well worth a visit for advice, assistance (including accomodation booking) and further information. *See the addresses at the end of this section.*

**Being there**

Of course, in giving you this overall guide of how to reach Donegal we've completely ignored all the wonderful landscape you'll be travelling through and not mentioned a single one of the excellent hotels, bars, restaurants and guest houses that lie on your route. We haven't given approximate travelling times because everyone likes to set their own pace and there's plenty to see and enjoy on the way to Donegal.

We've tried to give you the most straightforward routes but if you see some sun-speckled mountains off to your left, or a quiet green glen to your right, or even one of the many tempting bars then our advice is: *stop!* Get out and enjoy yourself.

*Relax, you're in Ireland, where time passes, but never flies.*

---

*Please note that we've done everything we can to be as accurate in compiling these details but timetables do change, trains get cancelled and coaches don't run, so always check when booking and check locally on your travel arrangements.*

**Bord Fáilte (Irish Tourist Board)**
Derry Road, Letterkeny, Co. Donegal, Ireland
(074-21160)
8 Bishop Street, Derry (0504-369501)
53 Castle Street, Belfast, BT1 1GH (0232-327888)
Tourist information points at:
McIntyre's, Ballybofey; The Diamond, Donegal Town; Folk Village, Glencolumbkille; General Stores, Glenties.

**Northern Ireland Tourist Board**
St Anne's Court, North Street, Belfast BT1 1ND
(0232-246609)

**Bus Éireann**
Busaras, Store Street, Dublin, Ireland
(01-366111)
Bus Office, Letterkenny, Co. Domegal, Ireland
(074-21309)
McDiarmada Station, Sligo, Co. Sligo, Ireland
(071-60066)

**Ulsterbus**
Milewater Rd , Belfast 3, N Ireland
(0232-333000)
Larne enquiries office (0574-272345)

**"The Swilly Buses"**
Londonderry and Lough Swilly Railway Co. Ltd.
Passenger Depot, Foyle Street, Derry, N Ireland
(0504-262017

**Iarnród Éireann**
Travel Centre, 35 Lr. Abbey Street, Dublin
(01-7034083/363333)

**Northern Ireland Railways**
Central Station, East Bridge Street, Belfast 1, N Ireland. (0232-230310)
Larne Harbour, Travel Centre (0574-270517)

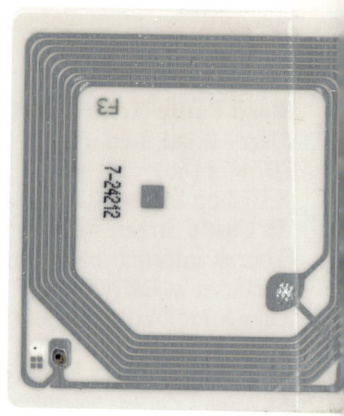

## MEMORIES

The Summer's light is glinting on a thousand silver rills,
The gorse and heath are blooming o'er moorland lone and distant hills.
But let the skies be dark or bright, or mist surround the mountains tall,
The hearts are fond and warm and light that call us back to Donegal.

*quoted from an excursion arrangements publicity leaflet issued by the County Donegal Railways Joint Committee for the summer season of 1957*